Edible Art

Tricks & Tools for Master Centerpieces from Carved Vegetables

Narahenapitage Sumith Premalal De Costa

D1119468

4880 Lower Valley Road, Atglen, PA 19310 USA

Other Schiffer Books on Related Subjects
Food Art: Garnishing Made Easy John Gargone
The Art of Food Sculpture Yuci Tan

Published by Schiffer Publishing Ltd.
4880 Lower Valley Road
Atglen, PA 19310
Phone: (610) 593-1777; Fax: (610) 593-2002
E-mail: Info@schifferbooks.com

For the largest selection of fine reference books on this and related subjects, please
visit our web site at **www.schifferbooks.com**
We are always looking for people to write books on new and related subjects. If you
have an idea for a book please contact us at the above address.

This book may be purchased from the publisher.
Include $3.95 for shipping.
Please try your bookstore first.
You may write for a free catalog.

In Europe, Schiffer books are distributed by
Bushwood Books
6 Marksbury Ave.
Kew Gardens
Surrey TW9 4JF England
Phone: 44 (0) 20 8392-8585; Fax: 44 (0) 20 8392-9876
E-mail: info@bushwoodbooks.co.uk
Website: www.bushwoodbooks.co.uk
Free postage in the U.K., Europe; air mail at cost.

Copyright © 2006 Schiffer Publishing Ltd.
Library of Congress Control Number: 2006925102
Original edition *Essbare Tischekorationen Zum Selbermachen*, Heel Verlag
Translated from German by Edward Force

Photos: Help, Helge Pohl
Publisher's Reader: Caroline Klaen
Setup and Layout: Herbert Menzel, Koblenz

Responsible for the contents: Narahenapitage Sumith Premalal De Costa, who
can be contacted through Triangle Hill Metalwaren GmbH, Friedenstr. 98, 42699
Solingen, Germany

Responsible for the text: Thishan Narahenapitage, Sithy Zaveena Jainudeen

Covers designed by Bruce Waters

ISBN: 0-7643-2513-2
Printed in China

EDIBLE ART

Tricks & Tools for Master Centerpieces from Carved Vegetables

I thank Ms. Christine Kelch, Business manager of the Hill Metal Goods Company, for her technical cooperation and the development of the cutting tools. Her ideas and involvement have contributed significantly to the success of the book.

Thanks are likewise due to my boss and the business Manager of the Aubergine und Zucchini firm, Ms. Silke Schnapp. She gave me the necessary space, both organizational and personal.

Hearty thanks also go to the Handelshof for the beautiful vegetables and photogenic fruits.

Last, but not least, I thank my wife, Sithy Zaveena, and my sons, Tishan and Heshan, who not only accomplished a great deal of writing work but also showed much patience.

The whole process was superbly coordinated and organized by my colleagues of the Heel publishing house. It was really pleasant to work together with all of them.

CONTENTS

FOREWORD

Finally it is here! The successor to the prize-winning book, *Too Good To Eat*. This book deals specifically with plate and table decorations that you can make. You will find out how simple it is to amaze your guests with little decorations.

All that you need is a bit of capability and the right tools. Very often, though, a store-bought sharp kitchen knife is sufficient to work on vegetables and fruits. For more impressive creations, one or another special tool is indispensable. Again and again, enthusiastic readers of my first book have called to ask where such an implement can be found.

A great portion of my equipment, though, is of the home-made type. In order to meet the demand, I have collaborated with Triangle® to develop an eight-piece set of carving knives, which has since been produced and marketed by the Triangle® brand. It includes all essential functions. Because of its clean workmanship, it can be used to carve fruits and vegetables easily and precisely.

This second volume of my work *Too Good To Eat* is intended not only for professionals, but also for hobby cooks who are just beginning to practice the modeling of fruits and vegetables.

Light objects with big effect should inspire even unpracticed cooks to try creating these vegetable centerpieces. Along with small plate and table decorations, this book includes more elaborate sculptures and showpieces, which are suitable mainly for buffets.

The special feature of the art of vegetable carving is that the materials which I use can be bought at the supermarket or weekly produce market. Many small decorations that I make are formed, in part, from the leftovers that I keep when I carve larger sculptures and showpieces. For example, from a melon rind, which otherwise would simply be thrown away, I carve leaves for a flower bouquet.

I wish you many enjoyable hours and, above all, much success in carving these beautiful yet simple creations.

Narahenapitage Sumith Premalal De Costa was director and kitchen chef of the Aubergine & Zucchini Company at the Federal Institute for Medicines and Medicinal Products, Bonn.
He can be reached through Triangle

A LITTLE STORY OF ORIGINS

"The eye eats too!" I have made this old folk saying my motto.

It is very important to create lively arrangements that are not only admired by your guests but also eaten gladly, and are also healthful.

In my creations I have been inspired again and again by the works of art and the history of my homeland, Sri Lanka.

Sri Lanka (formerly Ceylon), the Pearl of the Indian Ocean, is famous for its carvings. This art is a part of its culture, which originated about 500 B.C.

Between the 14th and 19th centuries, the artistic handicraft of Sri Lanka developed further, and carvings of wood or ivory, as well as sculptures of silver or brass, were very much in demand.

The Grizzly masks of wood, brass, silver and ivory, which the island's inhabitants wore in rituals in those times, are very famous.

The brightly painted, devilish-looking masks symbolize characters and characteristics of various animals. These masks are still worn by devil dancers in southern Sri Lanka.

In the ethnological museums of Munich and Berlin, you can admire collections of masks from Sri Lanka.

In present-day Sri Lanka, the carvings have become more modern. Many hotel-keepers have meanwhile discovered that these carvings are very attractive to tourists.

Buddhistic household, as well as in Buddhist temples, the sacrifice of the "Gilan Pasa Pooja," in which the first portion of every meal or drink is intended for Buddha, is a daily practice.

The gifts are prepared elaborately as gifts to Buddha and decorated with splendidly carved fruits and vegetables. The bowl from which Buddha is supposed to take these gifts is also often carved from a fruit.

Meanwhile, European gastronomy has also discovered these exquisite vegetable carvings and developed the profession of the "Kitchen Artist."

Many cooks have transferred the historical models to fruits and vegetables. The art of vegetable carving in Sri Lanka has its background not only in artistic history. Religion also plays a great role: In almost every

TIPS AND TRICKS FOR SUCCESS

Fruits and vegetables are not only very important constituents of our daily nourishment, but with a bit of patience, practice and proficiency they can turn every dish, every table or buffet into a sensory experience of a special kind. Surprise your guests with artistic little plate decorations or artistic arrangements for a reception. From simple to complicated, from single pieces to bouquets—give your fantasy free rein.

Success depends not only on your ability, but also on the choice of the materials to be used, and naturally also on the suitable tool. The better the quality of the raw materials, the lovelier is the end product. Try to buy fruits and vegetables corresponding to the season. That is the simplest way to assure that the fruits are optimally ripe.

When choosing the materials, look for nice colors and be sure that the vegetables have no bruises. Those not only spoil the workmanship but also make the fruit spoil more quickly.

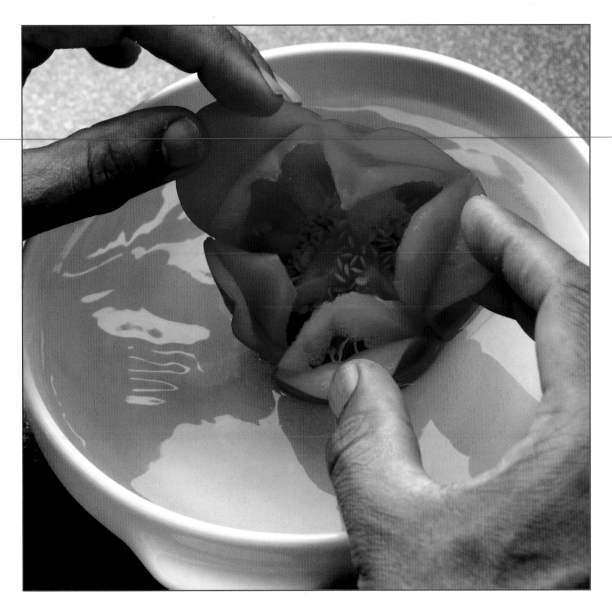

When you buy fruits and vegetables, look for firmness. The softer the material is, the more imprecise the cuts will become, and the pieces will also fit together worse. Always handle the piece with care, so as not to destroy anything, but hold it firmly so it will not slip from your hand. Not only could your work of art be ruined, but you might also cut yourself with the sharp implement. You should always avoid soft types of fruits and vegetables, such as bananas.

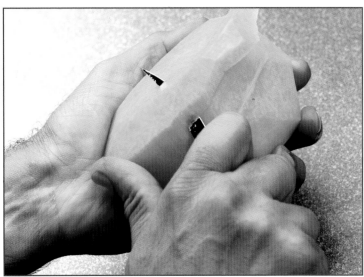

Firm types such as white and red radishes are particularly well suited to carving small objects. Tomatoes possess a greater degree of heaviness and should be worked only after some practice. For larger objects, melons are especially suitable. The varied palette of colors, from dark green to yellow, and their firmness invite you to try your skill on them.

Keep your carving material, particularly firm types from pineapple to zucchini, in the refrigerator until you work with them. After taking them out of the refrigerator, you should begin quickly.

Fit the material for your works of art together according to occasion and motif. Combine different types of fruits and vegetables and play bravely with the colors. Many arrangements come to life through inspired color combinations.

Make your choices not only according to the colors of the unworked materials. Remember also that many fruits have varied layers of color for you to use. Different colors can be exposed by different depths of cutting and indentation. This play of colors is most noticeable in a watermelon. Under the green rind there is first a white layer of fruit flesh before the red glows through. Make use of these colors, and work with varying cutting depths.

Before you begin your work, you should make sure that your implement is well sharpened. With dull knives you get bad and unsatisfying results. The risk of injuring yourself is also much higher.

Your work surface should have a comfortable height for you, and your workplace should be well lit. Sit relaxed and hold the knife loose in your hand. You should leave enough time for your work. When you guide the cutting tool like a writing implement, you can best control the direction and depth of the cutting.

Always have a container of ice water ready, into which you can immediately place the finished pieces. Thus they remain fresh until they are used, and delicate objects like flowers can "blossom." Styrofoam boxes filled with ice water are suitable for longer transport. If large arrangements for buffets are to stay fresh for a long time, spray them with ice water every half hour. The finished objects will also survive a night in the refrigerator.

I wish you lots of fun in your attempts!

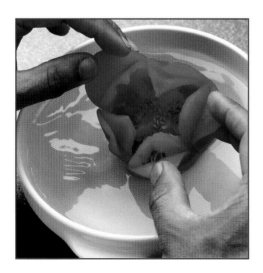

SEASONAL SCHEDULE

Fruit/Vegetable	Early Season	Height of Season	Late Season
Beet, red	July	August-November	January-March
Cauliflower	May-June	July-October	November
Cucumber	May	June-September	October-November
Carrot	June	July-November	December-February
Cabbage	May-August	September-November	December-January
Eggplant	June-July	August-September	October-November
Honeydew	May-June	July-October	November
Leek	March	April-November	December-February
Onion	May-June	July-September	October-February
Radish, red	January-March	April-August	September-November
Radish, white	April-May	June-November	December-January
Squash	July-August	September-December	January-February
Tomato	June-July	August-September	October-November
Watermelon	July	August-December	January
Zucchini	June	July-October	November

TOOLS AND KNIVES

To be able to create decorative and appetite-inspiring decorations out of fruits and vegetables, one needs the right tools.

Several of the most important implements and their possible uses will be shown on the following pages.

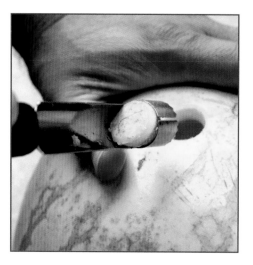

Apple Corer [1]

With the help of its sharp edges, the apple corer is twisted into the fruit at the stem and the core removed.

Large fruits can also be perforated with it, for example, in order to insert flowers.

Decorating knife [2]

2

The knife the cuts the well-known waved slices of red beets, cucumbers, and carrots can also cut butter and cheese into attractive shapes.

Fruit decorator [3]

If one cuts into melons or squash, for example, around their 'equator", one created two decorative zigzag-edged halves.

3

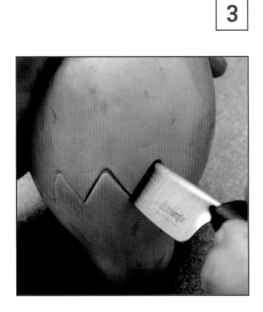

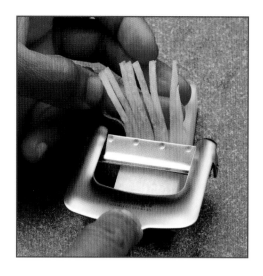

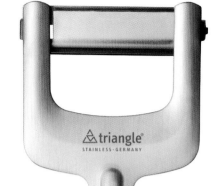

4

Julienne Cutter [4]

The julienne cutter serves to cut thin strips of carrots, zucchini, cucumbers and other not-too-soft types of vegetables.

Whether for garnishing or creating long vegetable spaghetti, its creativity is scarcely limited.

Potato Spiral Cutter [5]

Spirals of potato, radish, carrot and other hard vegetables will always astound your guests.

Twist the pointed tool into the fruit and draw it out with the finished spirals.

The hollowed-out fruit can, for example, be filled with fresh cheese.

5

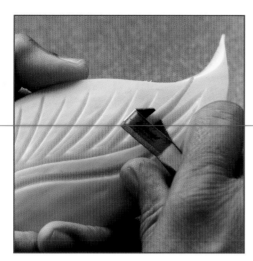

6

Kerf Knife [6]

With the notch knife, notches of varied depths can be created.

Small vegetables such as radishes can be worked just as successfully with it as squash.

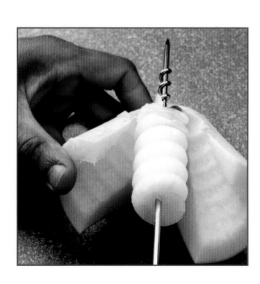

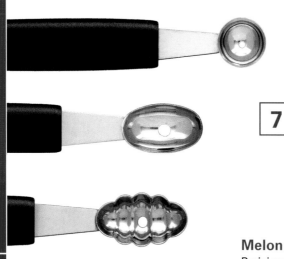

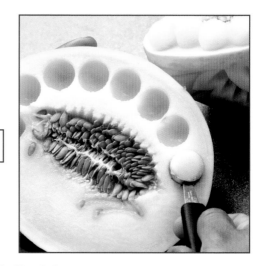

7

Melon baller [7]
Parisienne scoop, potato borer, ball cutter.

Small effort, great effect: Spheres of melon, papaya, mango, butter or potato (so-called "pommes parisiennes") are fun and make every food into something special.

The scoop exists not only in different sizes, but also in various shapes, for example, oval or waved.

Melon baller [8]

The "mini" scoop produces little pearls. It is especially suitable for decorating main courses and desserts. For cutting filigree shapes and figures, the pearl scoop is indispensable.

8

Spiral Cutter [9]

Like sharpening a pencil, radishes, carrots and other hard vegetables can be sent through the spiral cutter to turn out a spiral. Wonderfully simple with fascinating effect.

Decozester [10]

String cutter, string slicer, Julienne slicer
With its fine holes, thin strips, for example, of citrus rinds or chocolate can be cut.

11

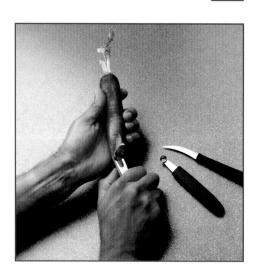

Canal Knife [11]

The chisel knife is used to peel fruits and vegetables of various hardness. Since it is drawn over the fruit and the depth of the peeling is defined precisely, using it is especially simple.

12

Swivel peeler [12]

Peelers are a must in every kitchen. No fruit can be freed of its skin more quickly and efficiently than with this tool.

The Triangle® Knife Set

The Triangle® knife set includes the special knives needed as basic equipment for working fruits and vegetables decoratively and professionally.

The variously shaped blades, hardened and hand-sharpened, make the working of delicate shapes and contours possible.

The handles, ergonomically shaped and equipped with soft grips at the front, guarantee secure handling.

All parts are washing-machine safe.

Cutting tools in a narrower sense

The **tall and small carving tools [A and B]** are made for such work as the creation of circular flower petals, flakes and ornaments. The smaller the diameter of these tools is, the finer are the shapes that can be created with their help.

The so-called **double V and V carving tools [C and D]** are indispensable for working out points, slim cuts and delicate patterns.

They were developed especially for creating filigreed leaves, delicate decorations and precise grooves.

With the **edged carving tool [E]**, flower petals and ornaments can also be created.

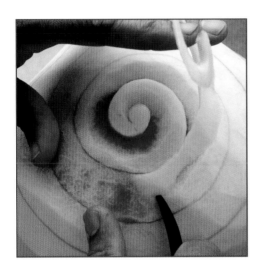

The **carving knife [F]** is the tool most often used and required for almost every decoration.

Its long, bowed blade, inflexibly ground to the point, allows precise cutting into skins, working out of bizarre shapes and continuing of complicated lines.

The **melon baller [G]** is the key to creating attractive spheres of papaya and other melons, potatoes, radishes and other types of vegetables.

The **ceramic stone [H]** has a special geometry that allows the sharpening of both rounded and pointed tools.

PLATE DECORATIONS

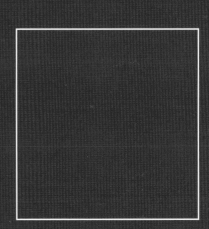

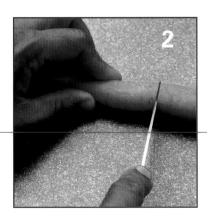 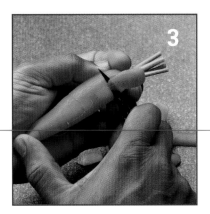 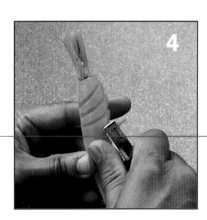

1.
Take a large carrot and cut off the top about three centimeters above the top of the shaft.

2.
Cut off the lower end of the carrot so that six to seven centimeters remain, with which you can work.

3.
With the **carving knife [F]**, cut the carrot back into its original shape.

4.
With the **kerf knife [6]**, cut spirals or a cubic pattern into the carrot.

Finally, the carrot greens can be decorated with parsley sprigs.

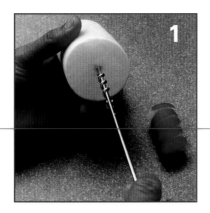

1.
Cut off a piece of a white radish about 6 centimeters long and stick the point of the **potato spiral cutter [5]** into the center of the cut surface.

2.
Twist it slowly around its own axis into the piece of radish.

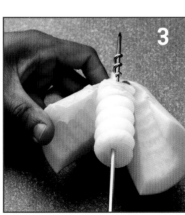

3.
When you have driven the spiral cutter through the radish, free it with two opposite side cuts. Thus you can remove the excess material in two halves, leaving the spiral free. Do not cut too deeply, as that could damage the worked piece.

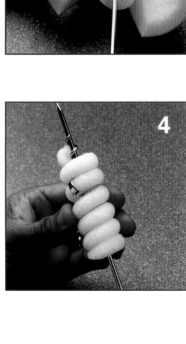

4.
Now turn the spiral cutter in the opposite direction, removing it carefully from the piece. For plate decorations you can use any kind of hard vegetable, such as red radishes, potatoes, cucumbers, zucchini, etc.

Now decorate the spirals with parsley sprigs or dill.

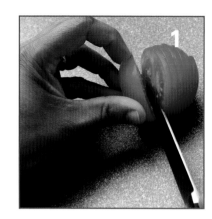

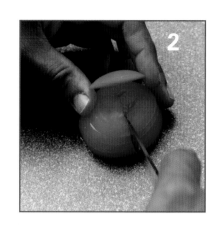

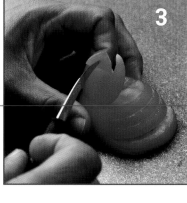

1.

Set a large tomato on its stem attachment and cut six parallel slices, equally thick.

Make sure that the slices are not completely separated from each other. The last piece can be cut off completely, to give the crab a base.

2.

Carefully raise the top slice, which will later become the crab's head, and use a sharp knife to cut the underlying slices through the middle.

3.

Cut a curved triangle out of the crab's head, giving our crab a face.

4.

Now carefully press on the crab's head, so that the individual legs spread out to the sides.

5.

With a pointed tool, make two small holes for the eye stalks, and insert a clove into each.

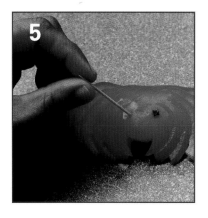

1.

Cut a slice about half a centimeter thick out of the middle of an orange.

2.

Take a cherry tomato and cut a cross into the skin with a sharp knife. Be sure that the flesh inside is not damaged.

3.

Very carefully open the individual petals with a **carving knife [F]**.

4.

Now set one or more cherry-tomato flowers on the orange slice.

You can also decorate the arrangement with parsley or dill sprigs.

1.

Remove the leaves from a white radish, so that you retain a cylinder about 25 centimeters in diameter. Cut pieces off all around the piece, giving it a hexagonal shape.

2.

Cut a long channel along the whole length of each side with the **kerf knife [6]** or **canal knife [11]**.

3.

Now insert the radish, point first, into the **spiral cutter [9]**. Hold the tool firmly in one hand and turn the piece as if you were sharpening a pencil.

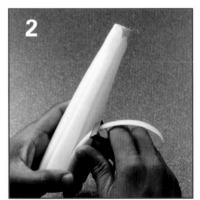

4.
Turn it evenly and without stopping, so that garland will not be torn.

In addition to radishes, you can use other firm vegetables such as carrots and thus combine the colors.

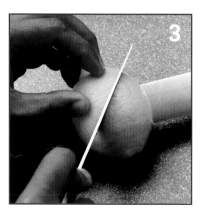

1.
Place the lemon with its point on the table and hold it firmly. Push a sharp knife into the center and through the fruit, and cut on down to the work surface.

2.
Lay the fruit on its side and place a knife with a wide blade, like the serrated knife shown here, in the cut. With the knife you used before, cut diagonally through the middle of the lemon down to the knife blade.

3.
Turn the lemon to its other side and make the same cut as before.

4.
Finally, take the wide knife out carefully. If the cuts were made correctly, the pieces will fall apart automatically.

Prop the two puzzle pieces up on a plate with a sprig of parsley, and strew small bits of zucchini around them.

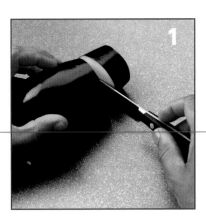

1.
You need a section of an eggplant about 5 centimeters long.

2. Hold the **carving knife [F]** like a pencil and stick it in about half a centimeter under the outside of the rind. Now cut down in a straight line, and end the cut about half a centimeter above the lower rind.

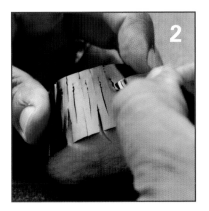

In a second work process, cut down about 2 centimeters from the upper edge, break the cut for about one centimeter, and then continue it in the same line to the lower edge.

Repeat the two work processes alternately until you have worked all the way around the piece.

3 and 4.
With a sharp knife, cut carefully around the inside of the rind, so you can remove the entire flesh in one block.

This flexible ring can also be used for other table decorations. If you prefer a different color, simply use a yellow or green zucchini.

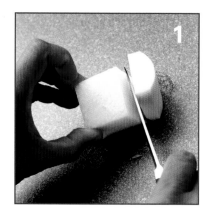

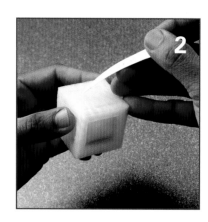

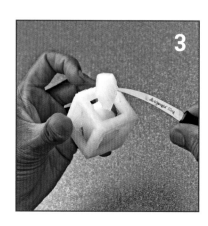

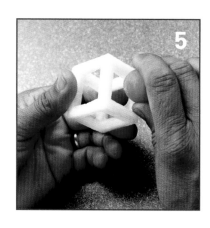

1.
To create a nice color contrast, it is best to use a white radish in combination with a carrot.

Cut a slice of a white radish, about 4 centimeters thick. Form it into a cube with equal side lengths of 4 centimeters.

2.
Mark a small square on each side of the cube with a **carving knife [F]**. Be sure that there is sufficient distance from the edges.

3.
Now remove the flesh from inside the frame, piece by piece. When you remove it, make sure that the edges are not damaged. Gradually the block will take on the form of a cubic cage.

4.
With the help of a **melon baller [7]**, cut a sphere from a carrot, ideally with a slightly greater diameter than the openings in the cage.

5.
Push the carrot sphere carefully into the cage.

Tip:
For somewhat practiced fingers: You can also make the sphere out of the material in the cage instead of cutting it out. The carving is, to be sure, much more demanding, and there is no resulting color contrast.

6.
As a decorative base for this model, you can use an eggplant napkin ring, the instructions for making which are found on pages 42 and 43.

Lay it on a plate and carefully press it flat. Set the cage with the captured sphere into it decoratively.

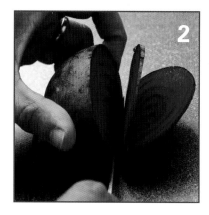

1.

Cut a red beet in half and cut one of the halves about 2 millimeters deep parallel to the outside.

Make sure that you do not continue the cut quite to the end, but leave some 3 millimeters as a connection.

2.

Repeat the whole procedure, and this time continue the cut all the way to the end, so that you create two connected slices.

3.

Lay the connected slices on the work surface and use the cutting knife to remove about a quarter circle on the open side. Round off the resulting angle. The connection must not be damaged here or in the further steps.

4.

Let the object lie flat on the work surface, and create the edges of the wings with two curving cuts.

5.

Lighten the wing surfaces by cutting two long curved areas into them and carefully removing the pieces.

6.

Now take the object in one hand and carefully spread out the wings with the other. Stick the lower parts of the antennae in firmly between the wings.

Attach the butterfly to a flower with the help of a toothpick. Directions for making various flowers can be found in the buffet decoration section, beginning on page 106.

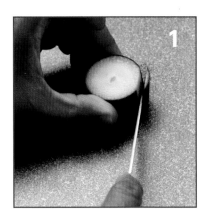

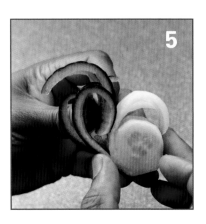
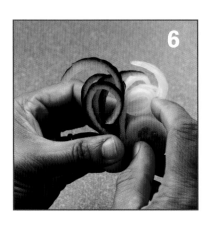
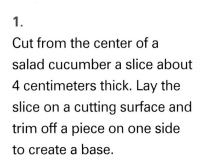
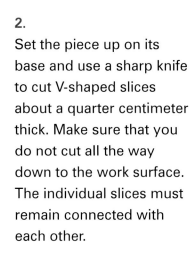

1.

Cut from the center of a salad cucumber a slice about 4 centimeters thick. Lay the slice on a cutting surface and trim off a piece on one side to create a base.

2.

Set the piece up on its base and use a sharp knife to cut V-shaped slices about a quarter centimeter thick. Make sure that you do not cut all the way down to the work surface. The individual slices must remain connected with each other.

3.
Now cut the rind off in one piece, starting from the base. But leave about 1 centimeter of the rind before you have cut all around the piece.

4.
Now make just as thin cuts into the flesh, again leaving about one centimeter uncut.

5 and 6.
First roll the rind strips, then the flesh strips, toward the inside.

1.

First cut off a slice from the tomato, with the stalk end, so that the object has a base on which it can stand steadily.

Now take a sharp knife and make a clean cut very carefully from the upper right, and then from the upper left, producing a V shape.

2.

Parallel to this V, now cut again. It is important to make the cuts neatly, for otherwise the individual pieces cannot be pushed apart properly.

3.

After about the fourth V cut, repeat the process also on the sides of the tomato, cutting V shapes there as well.

4.

Now place the object on the work surface and carefully push the central V sections apart like a fan with your finger.

Fan out the side elements in the opposite direction.

1.

Out of a squash, cut an oval piece 15 centimeters long and about 6 cm wide, and cut off a thin piece on one side, so as to make a base. Cut the piece crudely into a fish shape with a **carving knife [F]**.

2.

In order to separate the head clearly from the tail, carve a waist and give the head a rounded shape.

3.

For the eyebrows, cut two big parallel arches on each side. Then cut away the flesh to the outside, following the arch, so that the brows will project clearly.

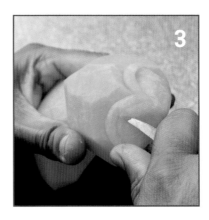

4.
Under the eyebrows, where the eyes should be, cut two small holes with the **small, round carving tool [B]**, and insert pieces of eggplant, which you previously prepared with the same knife.

5.
With the **tall, round carving tool [A]**, cut the scales in rows, forming a large arch going diagonally downward behind each of the brows.

6.
After finishing each row, use a **carving knife [F]** to cut a strip of flesh away along the arched row, so the scales project three-dimensionally.

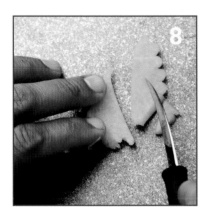

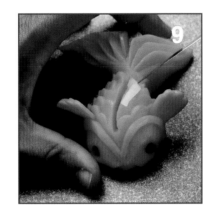

7.
Carve the tailfins with the cutting knife.

8.
Out of a squash cube measuring four centimeters, cut out three slices each half a centimeter thick. Put one slice atop another for each side fin and carve the fin shape. Decorate the edges by using the small, arched cutting knife.

The back fin will be made out of the third slice, and should be longer and thinner than the side fins.

9.
Using the **canal knife [11]**, cut a deep groove the length of each side, and one on top of the back.

10.
Now insert the side fins and the back fin into these

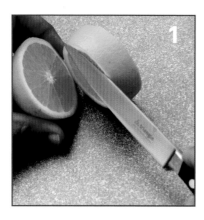

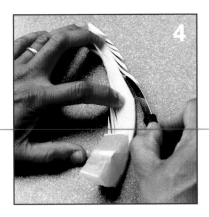

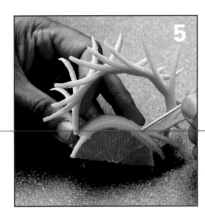

1.

Cut both ends off an orange or a lemon, so that you have a disc about 2 centimeters thick.

2.

Loosen the rind almost all around in one piece, but leave one to two centimeters in place.

3.

Cut the disc in half, and use only the disc with the rind attached to it.

4.

Put the piece on its "back" and hang onto the strip of rind. On both sides, make thin diagonal cuts into the rind.

5.

Turn the side with the attached rind upward and bend the rind back in a bow. Use toothpicks to attach the arched rind to the orange.

Now you can decorate the citrus king with flowers—you will find a thorough description of how to make a filigreed blossom on pages 112 ff.—or fine strips of rind.

6.

Such strips, as well as julienne cuts—you will find instructions on page 61— can also be used as an added decorative element. Unlike juliennes, strips are not cut, but scraped, and are shorter and curved.

You can use materials such as the firmer fruits, like lemons. Draw a **decozester** [10] along the lemon rind with some pressure. The prepared strips fall off automatically.

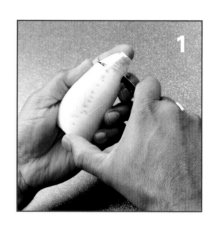

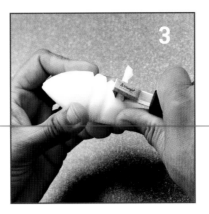

1.
Cut off a piece of a white radish some 7 to 8 centimeters long. This piece should come to a point at one end.

Peel it with a **carving knife [F]** and cut the piece into the shape of a bee's body.

2.
Insert a toothpick into the pointed end of the body as the bee's stinger.

3.
With the **kerf knife [6]**, cover the body with parallel horizontal grooves.

4.
For the eyes, make two small holes with a **small, round carving tool [B]**.

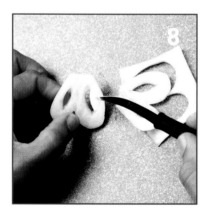

5.
With the same tool, take two suitable cylinders from an eggplant and set them into the prepared eyeholes.

6.
Cut another piece of radish, about 4 centimeters long, and place the cylinder on the cut surface.

Cut two slices, about half a centimeter thick, out of the middle.

7.
Lay one slice atop the other and cut out a heart shape for the wings.

8.
Now make two small, long oval cuts in each wing and remove the excess pieces.

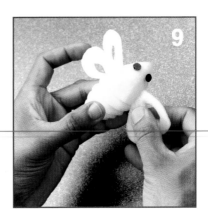

9.
On the right and left sides of the bee's body, make a slit that you can set the wings into.

These slits should be deep enough so that the wings will stay firmly in place.

10.
Cut a papaya in half and use the rounded half.
Start in the middle town the notch knife and lead it down to the cut surface in a narrow spiral.

11.
Attach the bee to the top with a toothpick.

12.
As a further decorative element, you can add long thin julienne strips.

For this, use a soft vegetable like a cucumber or zucchini, and draw the **julienne cutter [4]** over it.

For color contrast, you can use various vegetable skins and mix them.

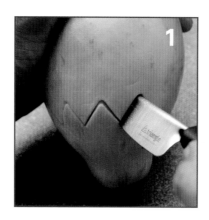

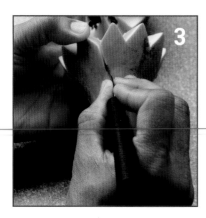

1.
Select a particularly large papaya. Stick the **fruit decorator [3]** deep into the fruit along its equator.

Pull it out, turn it around, and put it back in, thus making a zigzag line.

2.
Now separate the two papaya halves from each other very carefully. Use the tapering upper half and cut off the stem attachment to provide a base.

3.
From the top, make cuts parallel to the rind, some 3 to 4 centimeters deep, at intervals of about half a centimeter, so that the flower petals project outward.

Then make a cut downward, about one centimeter long and just as deep, between each of the individual flower petals.

4.
Cut about half a centimeter deep, in the form of a longitudinal petal, into each petal from outside, so that the big petals can "blossom".

5.
Now pres the small petals toward the inside and pull the large petals toward the outside with your thumb.

6.
The black papaya seeds are not edible but should not be removed, since they provide a nice color contrast at the center of the flower.

63

1.

Take a salad cucumber and cut off a thin strip along its entire length, so as to make a standing or lying base. Then cut about a quarter of the cucumber off straight.

2.

Lay the cucumber on its "belly" and cut a V-shaped notch on either side about three centimeters from the rounded end.

3.

Now cut four thin strips off each side of the body; work from the cut end toward the rounded one. There, though, the strips must remain connected with the cucumber body.

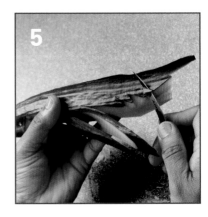

4.
Form the crocodile's mouth with two side cuts running together.

5.
Cut regular zigzags on both sides of the crocodile's mouth, as rows of teeth.

6.
Carefully separate the rind from the flesh with a horizontal cut, in order to form the upper and lower jaws.

7.
Cut short parallel grooves into the back with the **kerf knife [6]**.

8.
Now use the **small, round carving tool [B]** to cut out two cylinders where the eyes should be. Pull these out a little bit.

9.
Starting from the head, carefully bend the first and third side strips on each side to the back and attach them firmly.

10.
Make a tongue of the rind of a yellow zucchini and stick it into the crocodile's mouth.

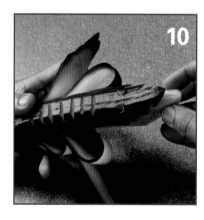

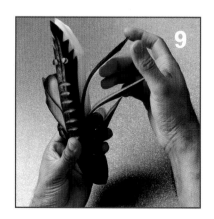

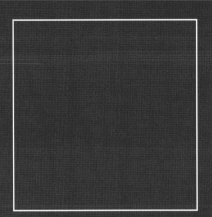
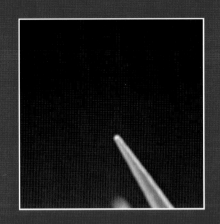

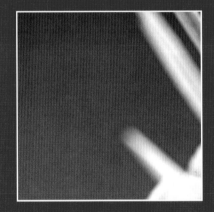

TABLE DECORATIONS

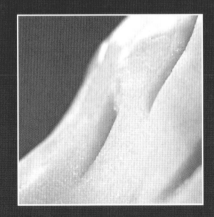

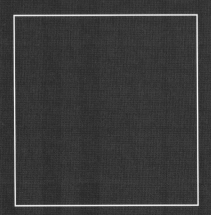
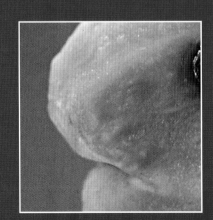

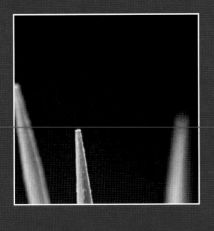

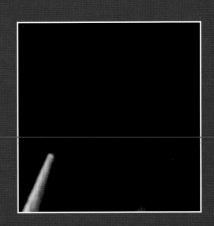
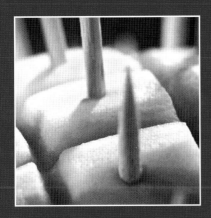

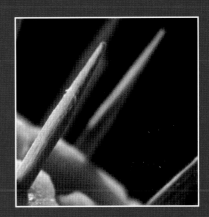
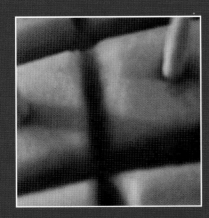

ELEPHANT WALK

White radish elephants with dark eggplant eyes go for a walk through the sprout savannas with radish and broccoli trees.

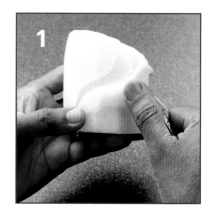

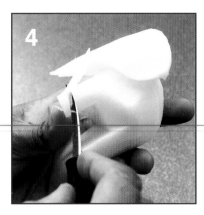

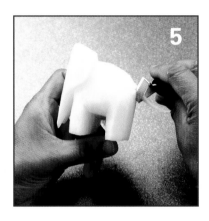

1.

Cut a piece about 10 centimeters long out of the middle of a white radish and peel it. Take the cut surfaces between your thumb and index finger. Now work with a **carving knife [F]** to carve the elephant's ears and trunk out of the piece.

2.

Then shape the back part and a round rear body.

3.

Carefully remove the excess material between the trunk and the front legs.

4.

Now work out the crude outlines of the front and hind legs.

The legs must be equally long, so the animal can stand well. Afterward, give the legs their final shape.

5.

Take **the kerf knife [6]** and draw it upward from the lower ends of the hind legs. Cut flat at first, and deeper in toward the top. Then the elephant's tail should stick out.

6.

With the same tool, carve short parallel grooves in the trunk.

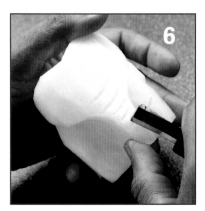

7.

Now separate the two front legs and the two hind legs from each other by cutting out a rectangle between each pair.

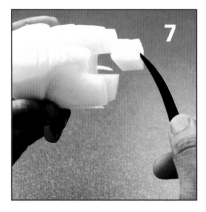

8.

With the **small, round carving tool [B],** cut out two small holes where the eyes will be placed later.

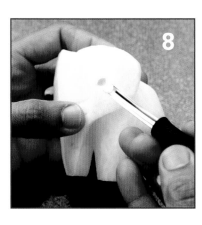

9.
Take two suitable pieces out of an eggplant and set them in as eyes.

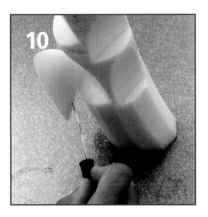

10.
Let the elephant family walk through a savanna landscape on your table.

Strew sprouts around as grass and plant radish trees. Then the elephants will feel just as much at home as your guests will.

Take a radish 30 to 35 centimeters long and peel off the green with a straight but, so that the finished tree will be able to stand.

Cut wide notches alternately on opposite sides of the trunk.

11.
Continue the steps evenly along the entire length of the trunk.

12.
Now take small rosettes of broccoli or romaine and stick them to the trunk with toothpicks.

WATER BUFFALO

The white radish water buffalo with eggplant eyes are dozing between chive reeds and flowers made of yellow zucchini and red radish.

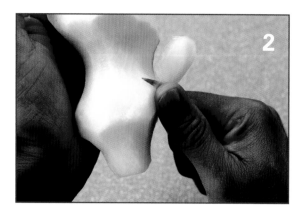

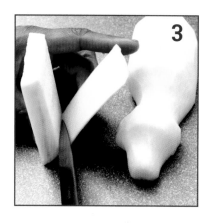

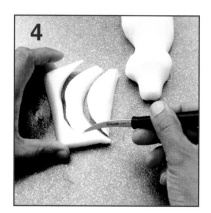

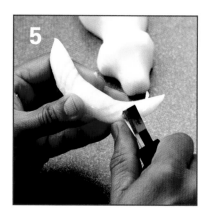

1.
Peel a piece of radish about 20 centimeters long, and then cut it in half length-wise.

Hold one half, with the cut surface, on which the water buffalo will lie later, down-ward in your hand and cut out, with the **carving knife [F]**, an arched area for the animal's neck.

2.
Now turn the piece first onto one side to cut out a neck arch, and then onto the other to repeat this step. Starting from the head, now shape the buffalo's body.

3.
Cut a slice about two centi-meters thick out of the middle of the remaining radish.

4.
Lay the slice down and cut the half-moon shapes of the horns out of it.

5.
Give the horns a structure by using the **kerf knife [6]**.

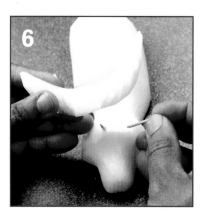

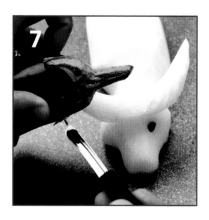

6.
Attach the horns to the buffalo's head with two toothpicks.

7.
Make two small holes with the **small, round carving tool [B]** where the eyes will be later, and set two cylinders which you have already punched out of an eggplant into the holes as eyes.

8.
Use the notch knife to make the buffalo's mouth as true to life as possible.

9.
With the same tool, make small, curving notches in the body, to represent the structure of a pelt.

Lay the water buffalo in a pan filled with water and create a luxuriant swamp scene out of chives, dill and parsley.

Put colorful little flowers and julienne strips in the water. If you want a truly realistic swamp, you can color the water with some sugar coloring.

Little flowers to strew

10.
For these little flowers you can use red radish or yellow zucchini. Stick a **small, round carving tool [B]** into the radish vertically about a quarter centimeter, and turn the tool around on its own axis.

11.
Now use the same knife to cut the tiny flower petals, by making individual cuts from the outside diagonally downward to the center of the flower. Lift the individual pieces out carefully.

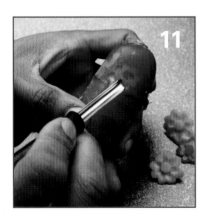

12.
Cut in somewhat diagonally from the outside around the center of the flower.

13.
Carefully lift the finished flower from the background material.

The colorful flowers described here can be used as added decorations in many arrangements, or simply strewn on the table.

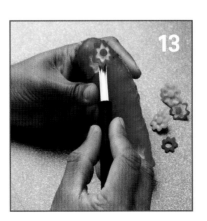

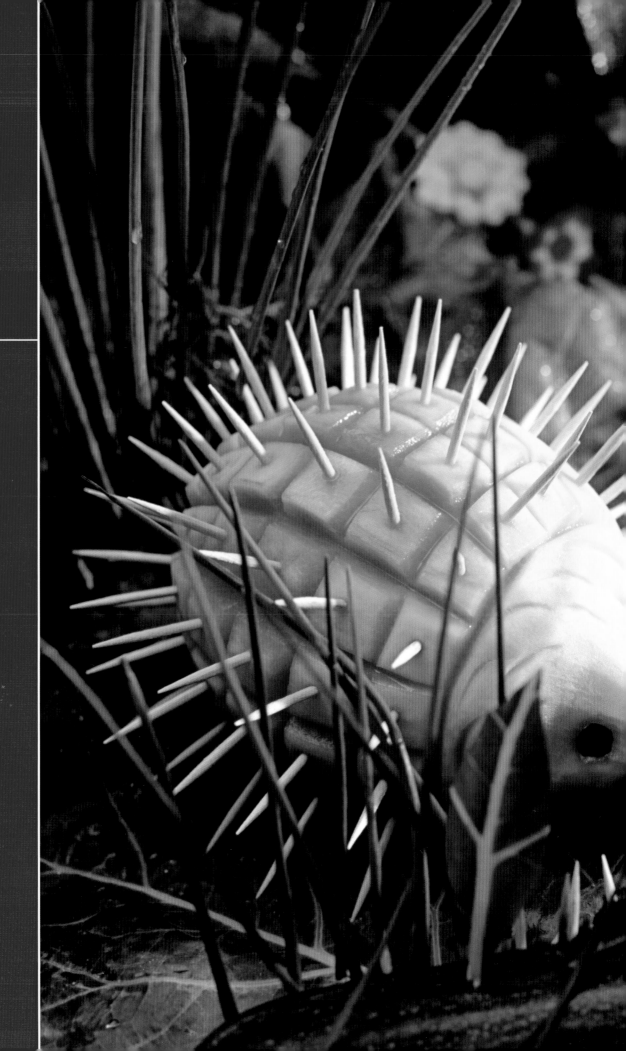

HEDGEHOG IN THE GRASS

The papaya hedgehog is armed with many toothpick quills. He crouches on kohlrabi leaves in chive grass, in the midst of many small flowers of red radish and yellow zucchini.

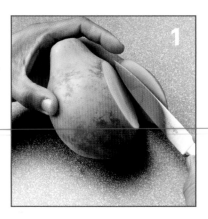  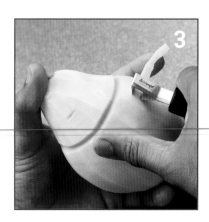

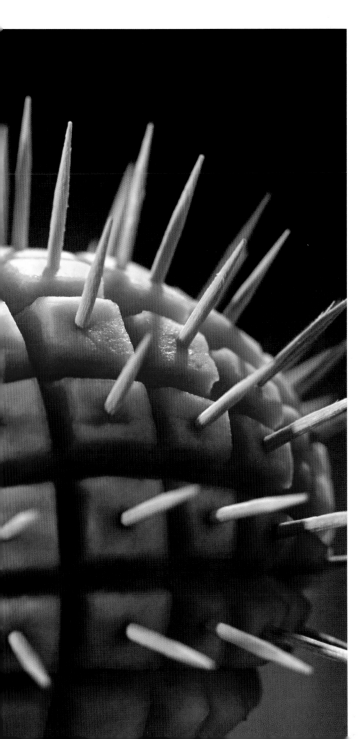

1.

Cut off a piece of a papaya, so the hedgehog can stand level later.

2.

Peel the fruit with a **swivel peeler of either kind [12].**

3.

Cut a notch around the fruit some 5 centimeters from the stem attachment, using the **kerf knife [6]**, in order to create a dividing line between the hedgehog's head and body.

Cut additional notches around the body at intervals of about 2 centimeters from the first one.

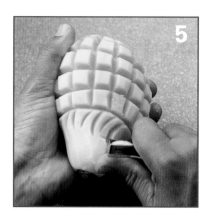

4.
Repeat this step along the
length, so that an even
checkered pattern results.

5.
With the **kerf knife [6]**,
make several small curved
lines in the face to simulate
hair.

6.
With a **carving knife [F]**,
give the hedgehog's face a
realistic shape, forming first
a "forehead" and then a
"snout."

7.
Stick in the **small, round
carving tool [B]** to make
two small holes, and stick a
clove into each to form the
eyes.

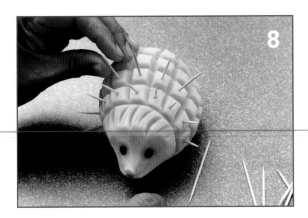

8.
Stick a toothpick into each of the small square surfaces between the grooves to form the quills.

To set the hedgehog artistically in the scenery, arrange him on the table in his "natural living space".

Set him on kohlrabi leaves and strew a few colorful flowers around him. Their description can be found on page 81.

9.
For the chive grass, cut a green zucchini in half lengthwise and stick several toothpicks into it here and there.

10.
Cut chives into pieces some 9 to 10 centimeters long, and stick the hollow chive stalks onto the toothpicks.

TOO GOOD TO WILT

The artistically decorated vase consists of a papaya. The small, almost transparent flowers are made of red radish, and their centers consist of lemon rind.

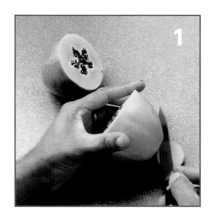

1.

Cut a papaya in half and cut a piece off the pointed end.

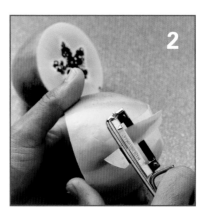

2.

Skin one half of the papaya, from cut surface to cut surface, with either type of **peeler [12]**.

3.

With the **kerf knife [6],** cut a groove all around, about a centimeter below the cut surface.

Under this groove, cut small semicircles in the fruit.

Be sure that the arches are the same size.

Now use the **edged carving tool [E]** to cut two wide and deep parallel grooves into the fruit, one centimeter apart.

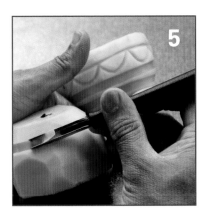

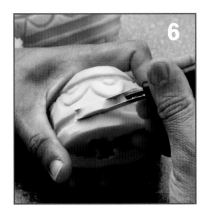

4.

With the **kerf knife [6]**, cut a meander pattern all around below the last encircling groove.

5.

Now take the other half of the papaya, cut off the pointed end, and peel this half.

Work with the **edged carving tool [E]** to make a wide, deep groove in this piece about one centimeter below the cut surface.

6.

Using the notch knife, cut arches going out from this groove. Fill each arch with a smaller arch. At the lower end of the ornamental band, cut a wide groove with the cutting knife.

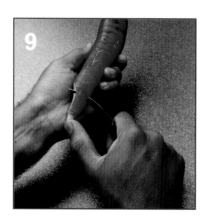

7.
Attach the two papaya halves to each other by sticking the two smaller cut surfaces together with the help of toothpicks.

8.
The finished vase can now be filled with a bouquet of fresh flowers.

Red-rimmed flowers made of red radish

For a luxuriant bouquet of fragrant, delicate flowers, the following type of flower is particularly well suited. The contrast of the red skin with the white fruit flesh of the radish makes this type of flower especially interesting.

9.
Cut oblong strips from a red radish, from above to below, on to the point. Turn the piece after every cut, and alternate the cut surfaces so that you have four or five cut surfaces.

10.
After that, cut parallel, half a centimeter above, to the previously made cuts. Be sure not to cut off the individual flower petals.

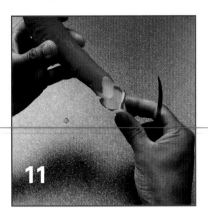

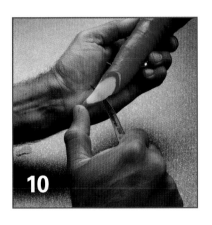

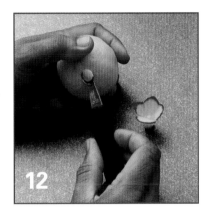

11.
When you have cut out the last flower petal, separate the flower from the remaining piece of radish with one cut.

12.
Using the **melon baler [8]**, form a hemisphere of lemon rind for the center of each flower.

13.
Attach the lemon hemisphere to the middle of the flower with a toothpick. Put the finished flowers in ice water before you decorate the vase.

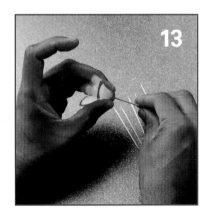

FRUIT BOWL WITH ZUCCHINI CUP

The exotic bowl filled with tasty little melon balls invites the guest to help himself. So as not to get his hands sticky, he can use the toothpicks that stand ready in the background in a cup made of yellow zucchini.

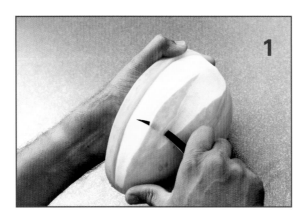

1.
Cut a melon in half length-wise, and use the **kerf knife [6]** to cut a groove about one centimeter below the cut surface and parallel to it.

Carefully peel this half of the fruit below this groove.

2.
With the same tool, now cut two semicircles, starting from the rim groove, into the melon about one centi-meter apart.

3.
Begin at a distance of two centimeters from the outer semicircle and, with a **V carving tool [D]**, cut notches toward it from below.

Make the cuts close to-gether, always along the outer semicircle.

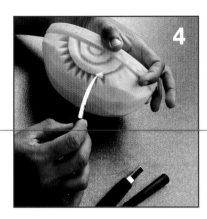

4.
Cut the separated pieces out with a sharp knife.

5.
Now repeat this process at a distance of about one centimeter, and then remove the remaining flesh with a **carving knife [F]**, so that the individual zigzags stand out clearly.

6.
Starting from the zigzag spaces, cut V-shaped rays into the fruit.

7.
After you have removed the pieces, cut out melon balls with a **scoop (7)** and finally put them back into the hollowed-out bowl.

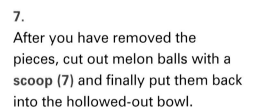

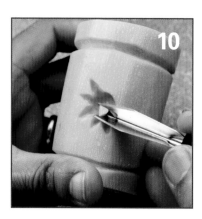

Toothpick cup made of yellow zucchini

8.
Cut a piece about 8 centimeters long from the middle of a yellow zucchini. Using the **melon baller [6]**, cut out a groove all around near the upper and lower rims of the zucchini cylinder.

9.
Hold the piece very carefully, and use a small pearl scoop (8) to cut a hemisphere out of the central area between the two grooves. Put the cutout piece aside.

10.
Using the **double V carving tool [C]**, cut a series of V-shaped rays about half a centimeter long around the cutout center.

11.
Use a piece of a toothpick to put the cutout semicircle back into the middle of the star. Now use the V knife to make a series of cuts somewhat further out, each one again about half a centimeter long.

12.
Use the **carving knife [F]** to make a circular cut around the star, and remove the superfluous material. Thus you make the star emerge two-dimensionally.

13.
Surround the star with small notches half a centimeter long.

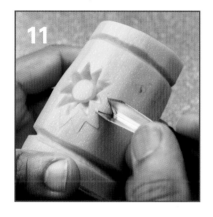

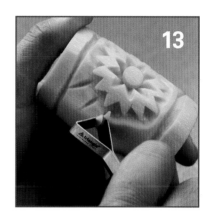

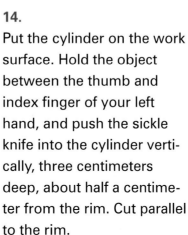

14.
Put the cylinder on the work surface. Hold the object between the thumb and index finger of your left hand, and push the sickle knife into the cylinder vertically, three centimeters deep, about half a centimeter from the rim. Cut parallel to the rim.

15.
Now hollow out the zucchini cylinder with a **melon baller [7]**. Afterward you can fill the cup with toothpicks.

NIGHT LIGHT

This natural and beautiful yellow lamp consists of a hollowed-out honeydew melon. A tea light burns inside the melon. The whole thing is decorated with leaves carved out of the rind of a green watermelon.

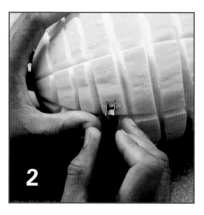

1.
Use a fairly large honeydew melon, one with good color.

Using the **kerf knife [6]**, cut eight grooves, equally spaced, from the top of the melon to the bottom.

Repeat this step by cutting horizontal grooves into the melon.

2.
Now take the **edged carving tool [E]** and cut small, deep rectangles out of the surfaces between the grooves.

3.
Form each individual rectangle with care and patience. You can also use a **carving knife [F]** to help remove the material.

4.
Cut the melon diagonally on its "back". This surface will serve later as its base. Carefully hollow out the melon over this cut surface, using the **melon baller [7]**.

Set the hollowed-out night light over a tea lamp, thus giving your table an impressive light. Place melon leaves around the glowing fruit, and an impressive table decoration awaits your guests.

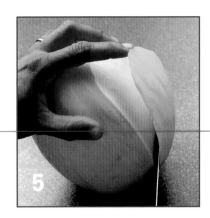

Leaves of melon rind—a honeydew melon is used here for illustration.

5.
Cut off a thick slice of melon rind. Be careful that the slice does not become too thin, because it could fall in pieces later.

6.
Lay the slice on the work surface with the rind up. Hold it firmly with one hand and work out a leaf shape with a **carving knife [F]**.

Hold the knife like a pencil, which helps to make your work even and properly proportioned.

7.
Use the **kerf knife [6]** to make two curved lines to define the rib of the leaf.

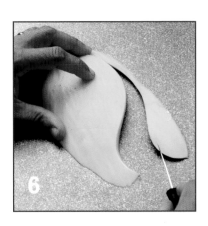

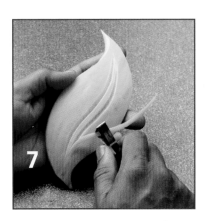

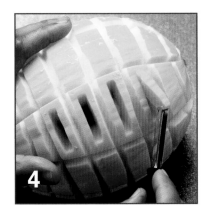

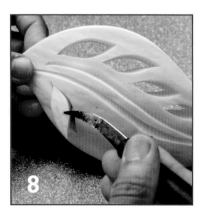

Starting with this basic form, you can make two different types of leaves, with pierced or relief patterns.

Pierced leaf

8.
Working outward from the rib of the leaf, make small curved cuts toward the outside. These cuts should follow the shape of the leaf and form small, long ovals.

Be sure to leave a sufficiently wide rib between the ovals. Then the ornament looks especially nice. Remove the material inside the ovals.

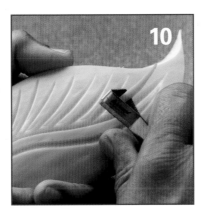

9.
Make cuts corresponding to the ovals on the edges of the leaf, to give it its final shape.

Relief leaf

10.
Working outward from the rib of the leaf, cut arched notches to the edge of the leaf, using the **kerf knife [6]**.

11.
With the **carving knife [F]**, cut zigzags into the outer edge of the leaf to give it its final shape.

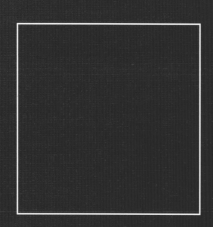

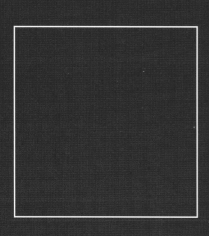

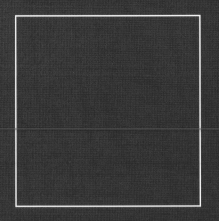

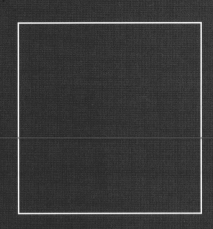

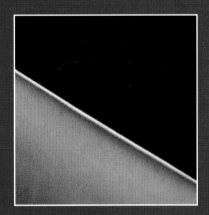

BUFFET DECORATIONS

REAL EYE CANDY

The flowers of this exotic arrangement were made of red radishes. The centers of the flowers are made of lemon rind. The vase itself is made from a dark green watermelon. A decorative frame is made of the leaves cut from melon rind.

1.

Take a large watermelon. About four centimeters below the stem attachment, use a **carving knife [F]** or a **kerf knife [6]** to make pointed oval grooves in the rind, following the curve of the melon.

Gaps of half a centimeter should be left between the grooves.

Use the knife like a pencil, so that you can control the depth and shape of the cuts better.

2.

Make arched cuts in the object, at intervals of half a centimeter, parallel to the edges of the arches.

The arches should proceed into the corners and enclose curved rectangular spaces.

3.

Work out this surface with a **carving knife [F]**, without damaging the thin rims.

The cutout areas form the background and the color contrast to the green ornament.

Repeat this step until you have covered the whole melon with an even ornamental grid.

Standing ring

4.

So that the melon will stand steadily, you can make a standing ring. Cut off the upper third of a melon. Cut a notch parallel to the rim, using a notch knife.

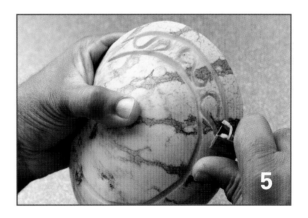

5.

With the notch knife, make a not overly wide ornamental band and cut off the upper part of the cap. Thus you make a ring in which you can stand the melon.

Flowers made of red radishes

6.
Take a red radish and cut around the lower point with a **canal knife [11].**

Make the cuts close to each other, and turn the radish after every cut. Be careful not to cut off the individual strips.

7.
Leave a stem about one centimeter in diameter in the center.

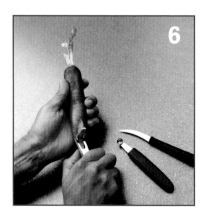

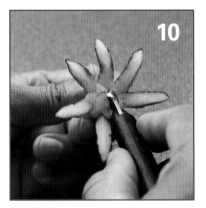

8.
With the **carving knife [F]**, remove the flower carefully from the stem.

9.
Form a hemispherical flower center of lemon rind, using the **melon baller [8]**.

10.
Take the flower carefully in your hand and, using the same tool, shape a flower center and set the small piece of lemon rind into it.

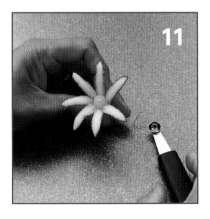

11.
Fasten the lemon piece in place with a toothpick, and put the finished flowers in ice water until further work, so that the flower petals can open farther.

Arrange the flowers on the melon and use them as a background and edge completion for the bouquet of relief leaves described on pages 105 ff.

EXOTIC FLOWER VASE

This sculpture in floral form is made from a watermelon. As further decorative elements, a white rose made of radish and two flowers made of squash and radish can be used. The artistic leaves are made of honeydew and watermelon rinds.

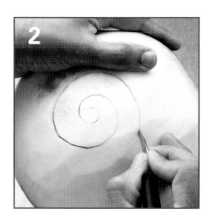

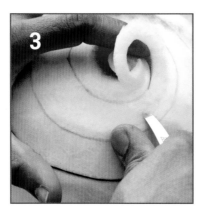

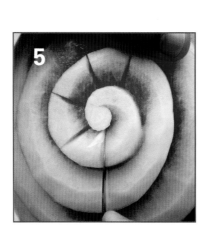

1.

Choose an especially large watermelon for this showpiece. Peel one half of the melon, best done with a fillet knife.

2.

Now cut a spiral into the melon, working outward from the center of the peeled surface, with a **carving knife [F]**. Hold the melon steady with your other hand.

You should hold the knife like a pencil. This helps to make the cuts even and correctly proportioned. The spaces between the individual spiral curves should always be about two centimeters.

3.

With a sickle knife, make cuts diagonally, parallel to the beginning of the spiral, and follow the spiral curve. Thus you expose a strip of fruit flesh, so that the spirals stand out two-dimensionally.

4.

After this step, the red fruit flesh should be clearly visible.

5.

Cut deep notches into the spiral, about two millimeters deep and at intervals of 1.5 centimeters. They should extend across the width of the spiral curve.

6.

With the **tall, round carving tool [A]**, make cuts diagonally downward to the bottom of the spiral between the notches, and lift the cutout material out.

7.

With the sickle knife, very patiently round off the corners of every individual flower petal.

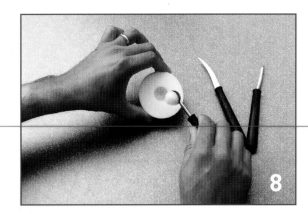

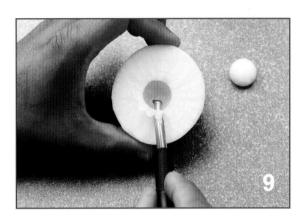

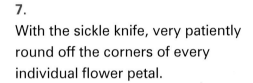

Ring flowers

8.

Cut a slice about 6 centimeters thick out of the center of a radish, and use a **melon baller [7]** to cut out a hemisphere in the middle of it. Put this hemisphere aside.

9. Stick the **small, round carving tool [B]** in diagonally around the cutout, about half a centimeter deep, to form the first row of flower petals.

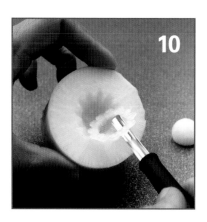

10.
Remove the excess fruit flesh.

11.
With the same tool, make cuts a little farther out, always parallel to the previous cuts.

12.
With a sickle knife, cut a ring around the circle of flower petals, and remove the resulting strips of material, so that the petals project two-dimensionally.

13.
Following the described steps, you can form a second, third and maybe a fourth circle of petals.

14.
When you have made the last circle of flower petals, carefully cut the flower away from the remaining material.

15.
Set the originally cutout hemisphere, curving upward, into the center of the flower and attach it with a toothpick.

16.
You can vary this flower form very simply by using any differently shaped knife instead of the small curved cutting knife, and using, for example, a squash or a red beet as the material.

Then simply follow, step by step, the directions previously provided for making the ring flower.

Rose

17.
Cut from the center of a white radish a slice four centimeters thick.

Hold the slice between your thumb and index finger, and use a **carving knife [F]** to shape it into an angled mass.

18.
Cut all around about two millimeters deep, parallel to the oval cut surfaces, making a flower pattern that becomes deeper toward the center of the piece, so as to afford greater stability.

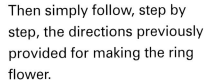

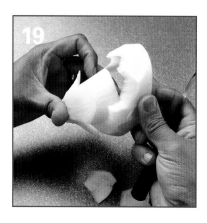

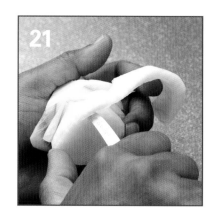

19.
Cut in vertically from above, about three millimeters from the rim of the piece, to the first row of flower petals, and peel all around. Remove the excess material. Be careful not to cut off any of the flower petals.

20.
Cut a second row of flower petals into the piece, alternating from the first row.

21.
As before, again cut away a thin area, three millimeters thick, behind the flower petals.

22.

Cut a third row of fruit flesh around the thus far undisturbed center of the flower, and thus give it a rounded shape.

23.

Hold the cutting knife like a pencil and cut out additional flower petals.

24.

If you need a rose-colored rose for an arrangement, cut a red beet and carefully brush it over the flower petals. You can, of course, also use food coloring.

25.

Attach the three different flowers to the melon with toothpicks, and arrange them as background ornamentation with relief leaves made of honeydew and watermelon. The description of these two types of leaves is found on pages 103 to 105.

TULIPS IN EVERY SEASON

A bouquet of colorful pepper tulips with chive leaves and bamboo stems provides the desired effect.

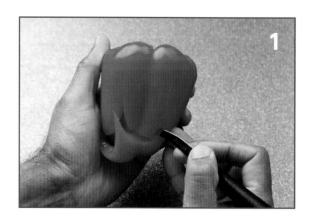

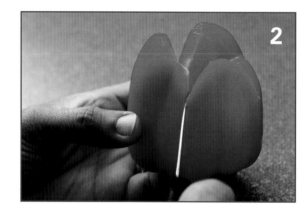

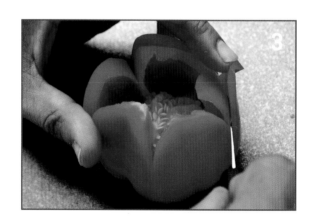

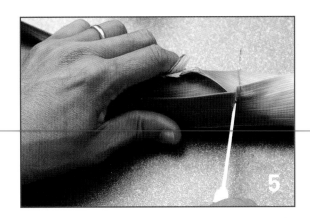

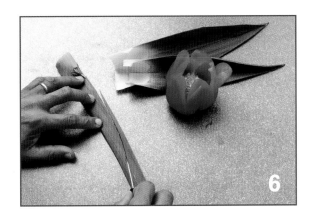

3.
With one neat cut, separate the rind from the fruit flesh for every petal down to the stem attachment.

The two resulting layers must not be separated from each other.

4.
Put the pepper tulip in ice water, so that the petals can unfold.

5.
Cut a chive stem off five centimeters below the green area.

6.
Separate the individual leaves from each other. Fold one leaf and shape it with a curved cut.

1.
Put the pepper in your left hand with the stem attachment upwards. With a **carving knife [F]**, cut the arched tips of the subsequent tulip petals opposite the stem attachment.

2.
Cut down some 3 to 4 centimeters between the arches to the stem attachment, in order to separate the individual flower petals from each other.

7.

Put one leaf over another and wrap the white lower parts of the leaves around a bamboo stick.

8.

Fix the leaves in place with flower wire at the desired height.

9.

Remove the stem attachment of the pepper and set the pepper tulip onto the stalk.